The Land of the Great Big "No!"

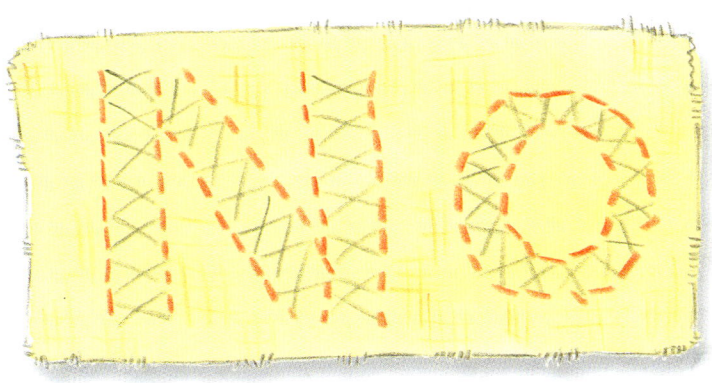

By Alan Trussell-Cullen
Illustrated by Mary Lonsdale

Dominie Press, Inc.

Publisher: Raymond Yuen
Editor: Bob Rowland
Designer: Mark Deutman
Illustrator: Mary Lonsdale
Cover Designer: Carol Anne Craft

Copyright ©1999 Dominie Press, Inc. All rights reserved. No part of this publication may be reproduced or transmitted in any form or by any means without permission in writing from the publisher. Reproduction of any part of this book, through photocopy, recording, or any electronic or mechanical retrieval system, without the written permission of the publisher, is an infringement of the copyright law.

Published by:

Dominie Press, Inc.
1949 Kellogg Avenue
Carlsbad, California 92008 USA

ISBN 0-7685-0316-7

Printed in Singapore by PH Productions Pte Ltd

1 2 3 4 5 6 IP 01 00 99

TABLE OF CONTENTS

Chapter One
"No! No! No!"   4

Chapter Two
Michelle Fights Back   6

Chapter Three
A Visit with the School Psychologist   10

Chapter Four
A Suspect Named "No!"   20

Chapter Five
Michelle Takes "No!" to Court   28

Chapter Six
Sing It! Shout It! "Yes! Yes! Yes!"   36

Chapter One
"No! No! No!"

Every time Michelle wanted to do something, someone always said, "No!"

"Can I have another cookie, please?"

"No!"

"Can I have a pet crocodile, please?"

"No!"

"Can I drive the car when we go shopping?"

"No!"

"Can I stay up late tonight so I can watch my favorite horror movie?"

"No!"

"Can I bake a chocolate raspberry marshmallow cake with licorice and peanut butter on top?"

"No, no, no, no, NO!"

Michelle was tired of living in the Land of the Great Big "No!"

Chapter Two
Michelle Fights Back

Michelle was still thinking of the Land of the Great Big "No!" when she went to school the next day.

In math class, she drew a bar graph showing how many times she'd heard people say the word *No*.

In art class, she painted a huge exploding **NO!**

During the writing period, she wrote a poem called, "Down with No."

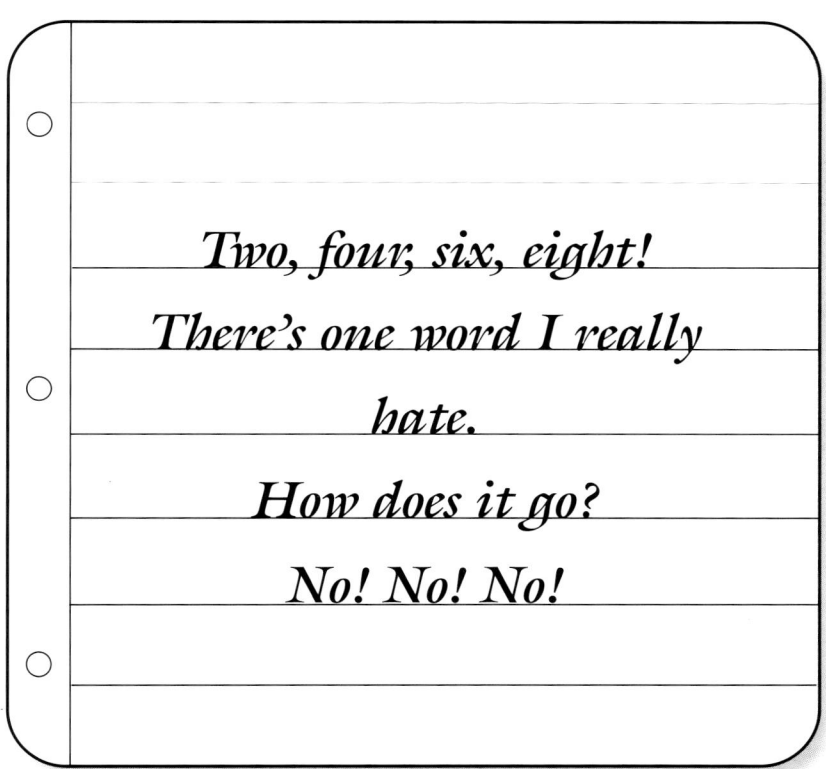

*Two, four, six, eight!
There's one word I really hate.
How does it go?
No! No! No!*

When her class went to the gym, Michelle made up her own little chant to say with the exercises:

"No more *No*!

No has to go!

We say No! No!

No more *No*."

In the afternoon, her teacher taught the class how to do embroidery. Michelle's teacher wanted her to make a pattern with flowers, like everyone else. Instead, Michelle made a pattern with the word *No*.

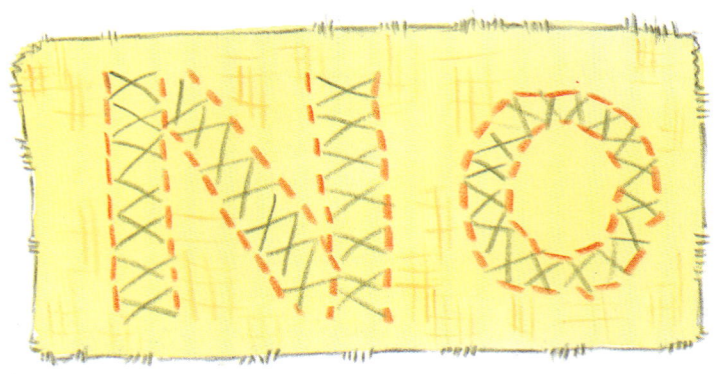

The teacher frowned when he saw it. The children all stopped talking and turned to look at Michelle.

"Michelle," said the teacher. "I'd like you to tell the class what your embroidery is about."

Michelle thought the meaning of her embroidery was obvious. She just shrugged her shoulders and said, "No."

The teacher was shocked! He told Michelle that she was being rude.

"Since you like the word *No* so much, you can stay after school and write an essay about it," he said. "I'll expect to see a full page on the word *No*."

So Michelle stayed after school that afternoon and wrote a whole page on the word *No*.

Chapter Three
A Visit with the School Psychologist

When the teacher saw what Michelle had done, he was furious. He was so upset, he sent her to the principal's office.

The principal looked at Michelle's paper for a very long time.

"She must be a very slow reader," Michelle thought.

"Hmm," said the principal.

"There's no letter *m* in the word *No*," Michelle said to herself. "Maybe the poor principal can't read very well."

The principal frowned. "Michelle," she said, smiling a faint smile. "I think I'd like you to have a chat with the school psychologist."

The school psychologist had a tiny little office under the stairs. She was writing when Michelle walked in.

"Sit down, Michelle," she said without looking up. She was using a very old pen that scratched along the paper.

Michelle sat down and looked around the room. She thought the school psychologist must like the color blue. The walls were painted blue. The ceiling was blue. There was a blue mat on the floor, and the school psychologist was wearing a blue dress.

Suddenly she put down her pen and looked up at Michelle.

"Hello," she said. And she smiled a wide smile that stretched from the long silver earring that dangled from her left ear to the long silver earring that dangled from her right ear. In fact, the smile was stretched so far, Michelle thought if she plucked the school psychologist's lips they would twang like a rubber band.

"Now tell me, dear, what's your favorite color?" she asked Michelle.

"Pink," said Michelle.

"Well, I can see there's a problem right from the start," the school psychologist said. "That's not the color most normal people like."

"And what color do most normal people like?" asked Michelle.

"Why, blue, of course!" said the school psychologist, and she smiled her wide smile again.

"Twang! Twang!" thought Michelle, and she grinned, which seemed to instantly turn off the woman's smile.

"Yes, well, I'd like you to take some tests," she said, opening a book filled with dark ink splotches. "Just tell me what you see in these pictures," she said.

"I can see they were drawn by someone who doesn't know how to draw!" said Michelle.

"No! No! No!" said the school psychologist. "You're missing the point. You have to tell me what you can actually see in the pictures. Like when you look at the clouds and you think you can see shapes of different things. So, what do you see in this picture?"

"It's obvious," said Michelle. "It says *No!*"

"And this one?"

"No!"

"And this one?"

"No!"

"And this one?"

"No!"

"And this one?"

"No!"

"And what about these?"

"No! No! No!"

The school psychologist looked at Michelle, shook her head, and said, "That's very interesting."

"No, it isn't!" said Michelle. "*No* isn't interesting! *No* is boring! *No* is annoying! *No* is infuriating! If I had my way, the word *No* would be banned! Even dictionaries wouldn't be allowed to print it!"

She paused to catch her breath and said, "They should lock people up just for saying *No!*"

"Ah," said the school psychologist. "If you want to lock people up, you've come to the wrong person. You'll have to go see the police."

Chapter Four

A Suspect Named "No!"

So Michelle went down the street to the police station.

"I've come about the word *No*," she said.

"I see," said the detective sergeant. "Do you mean it's missing? Well, you've come to the right place. The police are very good at finding things, you know."

"It's not missing," said Michelle.

"Then has it been damaged or hit over the head with something?" asked the detective sergeant. "The police are very good at dealing with things like that."

"It hasn't been damaged or hurt," said Michelle. "Though sometimes it feels like it's hitting *me* over the head!"

"Has it been stolen?" asked the detective sergeant. "The police are good at catching thieves, you know."

"It hasn't been stolen," said Michelle. "But I wish it had been!"

"I'll tell you what," said the detective sergeant. "Why don't you give me a good description of this word. Then we can have a sketch artist draw a picture of it and put it in the newspaper and on television. Then people will be able to report to us if they see it. So, what exactly does this word look like?"

"It's simple," said Michelle. "It's a word."

"But what kind of a word?" asked the detective sergeant. "Is it a big word, or a little word? How tall is it? Does it have any distinguishing marks or tattoos?"

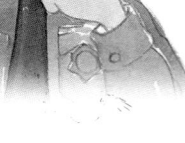

"For goodness sake!" said Michelle. "It's just two letters. An *N* and an *O*! People don't put tattoos on letters. And as for how tall–it can be as small as the small print at the bottom of a newspaper advertisement, or as big as a billboard!"

"Sounds like a tricky customer," said the detective sergeant as he wrote in his notebook:

May come in a number of disguises.

"And what has this word been up to?" he asked. "What sort of crime has it committed?"

Michelle looked up at him and shook her head. "What do you mean, what sort of crime has it committed?"

"You know," he said. "Has it robbed a bank or broken into someone's house, or failed to get a license for its dog?"

"It's annoyed me, that's what it's done!" she said, raising her voice a little.

"Ah," said the detective sergeant. "That's what we in the police department call"–and he wrote in his notebook:

Threatening with intent!

"And it *keeps* annoying me!" Michelle said.

"Ah," said the detective sergeant. "That's what we in law enforcement call"–and he wrote:

Intimidation!

"Everywhere I go, I hear the word *No!*" said Michelle.

"Hmm," said the detective sergeant, and he jotted down:

Making a public nuisance of itself!

"There ought to be a law against it!" said Michelle.

The detective sergeant looked startled. He took a deep breath, sat back in his chair, clasped his hands across his stomach, and frowned.

"Ah," he said thoughtfully. "If it's laws you want, you've come to the wrong place. We just catch people who *break* the laws; we don't *make* them. If it's laws you want to find out about, you'll have to talk to a judge."

Chapter Five

Michelle Takes "No!" to Court

So Michelle went to the courthouse to see the judge.

"Stand up before the judge!" said the judge's assistant.

"I *am* standing," said Michelle.

"Oh, so you are," said the judge's assistant. "You're not very tall, are you?"

"That's because I'm a child," said Michelle.

"Ha!" said the judge's assistant. "A perfect alibi."

And he led Michelle down the hall to the judge's courtroom.

The judge was busy cracking walnuts with his gavel when they walked in. His parrot, which was perched nearby, kept saying, "Quiet in the court! Quiet in the court!"

"I take him with me whenever I have a particularly boring case to hear," the judge explained. "With him around, I can take a little nap without anyone noticing. Now, what might your problem be, child?"

"It's simple, really," said Michelle. "There are too many *No's* in the world, and I think there should be a law against them."

The judge frowned. Then he walked over to his bookcase and took down a thick book of laws. Quietly, he began to turn the pages.

From where she sat, Michelle could see that he was holding the book upside down.

"We judges always read upside down," he explained. "We're always trying to get to the bottom of things as quickly as possible. And if you want to get to the bottom of a page as quickly as possible, why not start reading there right from the start?! It's sensible, don't you think?"

Michelle didn't know what to think.

"Now then," said the judge, checking the index in *The Big Book of Laws*, "laws against the word *No* ..."

"That's right," said Michelle.

"Nope," said the judge. "I'm afraid there are no laws against it. In fact, our laws are full of *No's*. No parking! No stopping! No loitering! No dogs! No cats! No talking! No fooling around! It goes on and on. No! No! No! No!"

"That's terrible!" said Michelle. "Why do we have to have so many *No's*? You should change all of those laws!"

"Did you say *change* the laws?" said the judge, scratching his head.

"Yes, I did," said Michelle.

"Well now, that's a tricky one," said the judge. "You see, we judges know all about the laws, and we make sure everyone obeys the laws. But we can't actually *change* the laws. Only the president can do that."

"Oh," said Michelle.

"You'll have to talk to him, I'm afraid," said the judge. "Next case, please."

Chapter Six
Sing It! Shout It! "Yes! Yes! Yes!"

So Michelle went to see the president.

"No, you can't go in," said the president's secretary when Michelle asked to see him. The secretary was frowning her most serious secretarial frown. In fact, she frowned so hard, her eyebrows almost met in the middle of her forehead above her nose.

"You have to ask me first," she said. "Then I give you an appointment and write it down in the president's appointment book. *Then* you can see the president."

"Can I please have an appointment to see the president?" Michelle asked.

"Impossible!" said the president's secretary. "He's completely booked up for months and months!"

Michelle could see the president's appointment book.

"Things to do today: *Nothing*. Things to do tomorrow: *Nothing*. Things to do the day after tomorrow …"

She had read enough.

"But his appointment book is empty!" said Michelle, stepping closer. "Look. Today: *Nothing*. Tomorrow …"

"I couldn't possibly comment on that," said the president's secretary. "You'd have to see the president himself about that."

"Good!" said Michelle. "So, where can I find him?"

"Through that door," said the president's secretary. "It's a good idea to knock loudly. That way, if he's asleep, you'll wake him up."

As soon as she walked into his office, Michelle could see that the president was having a very bad day. He seemed tired, and he had chewed off the ends of all his pencils. That was because all the other politicians kept criticizing him.

"I don't know what's wrong with the people in this country!" the president said.

"Ah! Now, there I can help you," said Michelle.

"You can?!" said the president.

"Yes!" said Michelle. "The trouble with all the people is that they have far too many *No's*!"

The president was stunned.

"Too many *No's*?" he said. "Goodness! I think you're right!"

He stood up from his chair. "It's all people think about! No, we don't want this law! No, we don't want that law! No, we don't want you to do this! No, we don't want you to do that! No! No! No! No!"

"At last I've met someone who understands!" shouted Michelle. She rushed up to the president and shouted, "YES!"

The president stood there, frozen, for at least a minute or two. Finally, he managed to whisper, "What did you say?"

"Well," said Michelle. "I think I said ... yes."

"Yes!" shouted the president. "That's it!"

"I haven't heard that word in a very long time," he said. "Say it again for me, please!"

"Yes!" said Michelle.

"And again!"

"Yes!"

"Whisper it."

"*Yes.*"

"Shout it!"

"*Yes!!*"

"Sing it!"

♪ ♪ "*Ye ... eeess!*" ♪ ♪

"Proclaim it!"

"YES!"

"Exclaim it!"

"YES!"

"I love it!" shouted the president. "Yes! Yes! Yes! I must call my secretary and have her tell everyone."

"Yes," said the president's secretary, and she smiled for the very first time in a very long time.

"Yes!" said the politicians. "We love it, too!" And they all stood and chanted:

"Yes! Yes! We love yes! Yes brings us all happiness!"

They were all so excited by the word *Yes* that they decided to proclaim a National Yes Day! On that day, everyone had to try very hard to say the word *Yes*. And all of the *No* signs were changed to *Yes* signs for the day.

Yes parking! *Yes* stopping! *Yes* loitering! *Yes* dogs! *Yes* cats! *Yes* talking! *Yes* fooling around! *Yes! Yes! Yes!*

In the schools, children wrote *Yes* stories and *Yes* poems. They did *Yes* paintings. Michelle's teacher was so excited, he asked everyone to write a whole page on the word *Yes*. And they did!

The next day, the people went back to saying "No" again. But somehow, they didn't seem to say it quite so often. And every now and then, someone would make a mistake and say "Yes," instead. Even Michelle's Mom ...

"Yes, you *can* bake a chocolate raspberry marshmallow cake with licorice and peanut butter on top," she said.

"I'll even help you!"